MOUNT RUSHMORE

by Thomas Kingsley Troupe

illustrated by Matthew Skeens

PICTURE WINDOW BOOKS
Minneapolis, Minnesota

Special thanks to our advisers for their expertise:

Ed Menard, Park Ranger
Mount Rushmore National Memorial, South Dakota

Terry Flaherty, Ph.D. Professor of English
Minnesota State University, Mankato

Editor: Shelly Lyons
Designer: Nathan Gassman
Page Production: Melissa Kes
Editorial Director: Nick Healy
The illustrations in this book were created digitally.

Picture Window Books
151 Good Counsel Drive
P.O. Box 669
Mankato, MN 56002-0669
877-845-8392
www.picturewindowbooks.com

Library of Congress Cataloging-in-Publication Data
Troupe, Thomas Kingsley.
Mount Rushmore / by Thomas Kingsley Troupe ; illustrated by
Matthew Skeens.
p. cm.— (American Symbols)
Includes index.
ISBN 978-1-4048-5168-9 (library binding)
1. Mount Rushmore National Memorial (S.D.)—Juvenile literature.
I. Skeens, Matthew, ill. II. Title.
F657.R8T76 2009
978.3'93—dc22   2008037905

Table of Contents

Welcome to Mount Rushmore National Memorial!
I'm William, a park ranger here. Mount Rushmore is
a beautiful symbol of freedom and democracy in the
United States. Let's learn its history.

The Lakota Sioux originally called
Mount Rushmore "Six Grandfathers"
before it was renamed.

Rushmore

Mount Rushmore is located in the Black Hills of South Dakota. While exploring in 1885, New York lawyer Charles E. Rushmore asked what the mountain was called. His guide suggested they call it Rushmore.

The Original Plan

In 1923, South Dakota historian Doane Robinson wanted to get people to visit the Black Hills. He imagined giant statues of heroes from the American West. The statues would be part of the rocky peaks in the Black Hills known as the Needles. Robinson thought Americans would travel to see the figures from U.S. history. In the beginning, his idea had nothing to do with Mount Rushmore. That would soon change.

Robinson wanted the face of Red Cloud to be carved into one of the Needles. Red Cloud was a successful Lakota leader from the mid-1800s.

But first, Robinson needed
to find an artist with a
grand vision.

The Sculptor

In August of 1924, sculptor Gutzon Borglum received a letter. In it, Robinson asked Borglum if he would like to make a "heroic sculpture of unusual character." Within a month, Borglum traveled to South Dakota to meet Robinson.

Borglum imagined carving figures from U.S. history. He drew sketches of his plans. Robinson agreed. But when Borglum checked the location, plans changed. The Needles were too weak to withstand the carving of large sculptures.

Some people did not want the Needles to be carved at all. They believed the natural rock should be left alone.

A Better Location

Borglum decided Mount Rushmore, just northeast of the Needles, was the best location for the monument. The granite there was strong enough for the work ahead. Mount Rushmore had one of the highest peaks in the Black Hills area. It also stayed well lit throughout most of the day.

"American history shall march along that skyline," Borglum said.

The granite on Mount Rushmore erodes, or wears away, only 1 inch (2.5 centimeters) every 10,000 years.

The Four Presidents

Borglum wanted to carve the faces of four U.S. presidents into Mount Rushmore. He chose George Washington, the first U.S. president. He also chose Thomas Jefferson, the third U.S. president. Jefferson wrote most of the Declaration of Independence in 1776.

George Washington

Thomas Jefferson

Theodore Roosevelt, the 26th U.S. president, was chosen because of his efforts to complete the Panama Canal. Borglum also chose Abraham Lincoln, the 16th U.S. president. Lincoln led the United States through the Civil War (1861–1865) and started the process that would end slavery in the nation.

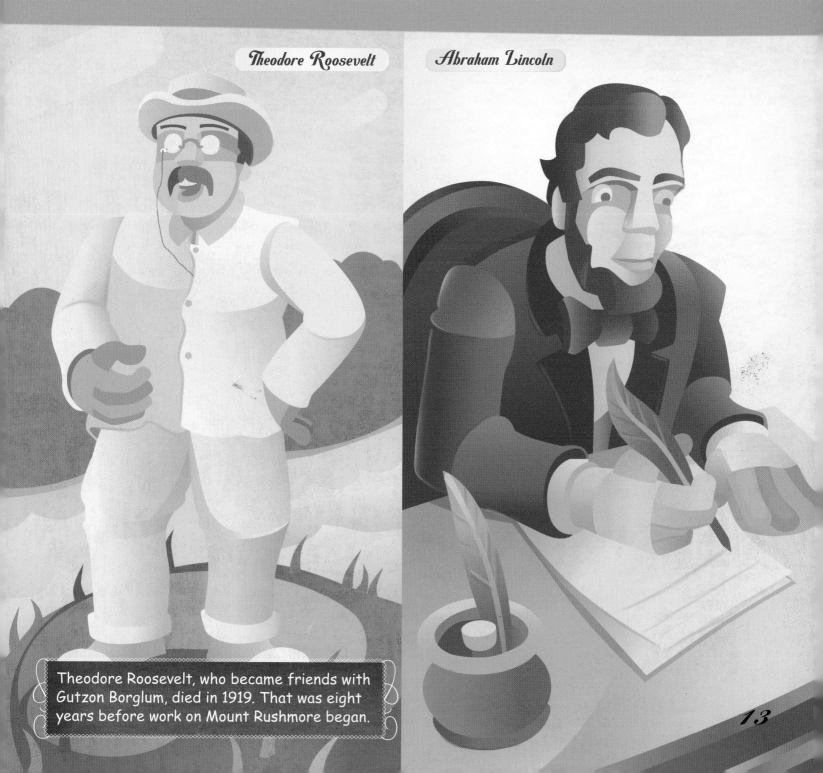

Theodore Roosevelt

Abraham Lincoln

Theodore Roosevelt, who became friends with Gutzon Borglum, died in 1919. That was eight years before work on Mount Rushmore began.

Kaboom!

After years of planning, the carving of Washington's face began on October 4, 1927. Dynamite was used to clear rock away from the mountain until just a layer of granite remained.

About 450,000 tons (405,000 metric tons) of rock were blasted from the mountainside. Today, the pieces are still scattered below the carved faces.

The last layer of rock was worked away using a process called honeycombing. Workers drilled holes 1 to 6 inches (2.5 to 15.2 cm) deep and about 1 inch (2.5 cm) apart. Then they shaped the stone using very sharp hand tools.

Mountain Carvers

Although Borglum was a famous sculptor, he didn't carve the faces of Mount Rushmore. Instead, crews of men were hired to shape the rock.

The work was often difficult. The summer sun made the granite very hot to work with. During winter, the men worked until severe cold forced them to stop.

More than 400 people worked on Mount Rushmore.

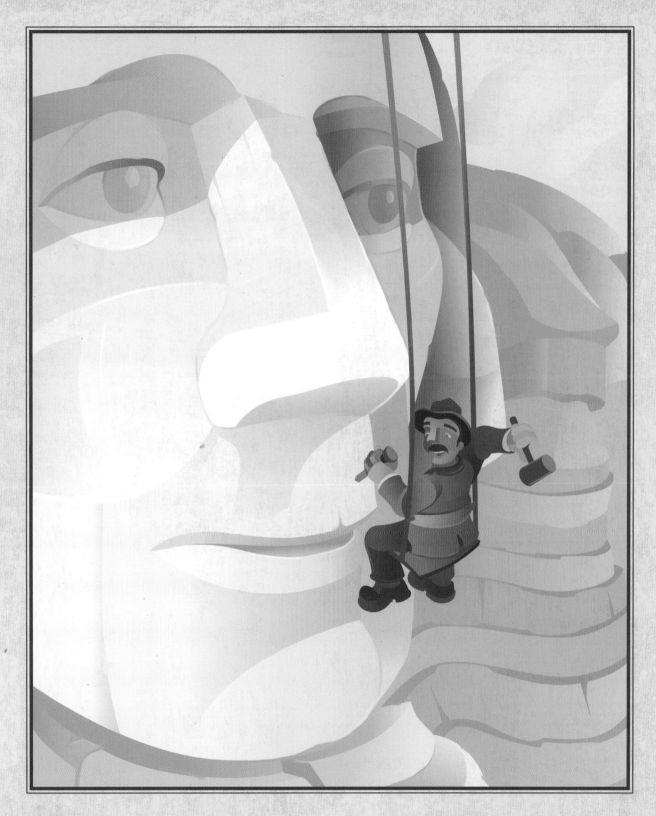

Workers also faced many dangers. They had to use dynamite. At times, they dangled from the mountainside while using tools that weighed nearly 60 pounds (27 kilograms)! The work was tough and dangerous, but the pay was good at the time. A carver was paid $1.25 an hour.

Dedication

The sculpture of George Washington was dedicated on July 4, 1930. That was two years and nine months after work on Mount Rushmore began.

Women from Rapid City, South Dakota, sewed a giant flag to cover Washington's face until it was revealed at the dedication. It measured 39 feet (11.9 meters) by 70 feet (21.4 m)!

Thomas Jefferson's sculpted face was dedicated in August 1936. President Franklin Roosevelt was in attendance. On September 17, 1937, the sculpture of Abraham Lincoln's face was dedicated. The date marked the 150th anniversary of the U.S. Constitution. Theodore Roosevelt's sculpted face was dedicated on July 2, 1939.

Looking Over the Land

In March of 1941, Gutzon Borglum died. His son, Lincoln, was asked to oversee the work on Mount Rushmore.

Because money ran out, work on Mount Rushmore ended on October 31, 1941. The entire project took 14 years and cost nearly $1 million to complete. Despite the dangerous work, not one worker died during the sculpting of Mount Rushmore.

Each of the Mount Rushmore faces is more than three times taller than the Statue of Liberty's face. Each president's face is 60 feet (18.3 m) tall. The Statue of Liberty's face is 17 feet (5.2 m) tall.

Mount Rushmore now has nearly 3 million visitors each year. It is a symbol of freedom and democracy. It also reminds us of the American spirit. It proves that not even a mountain can stop a grand vision!

I hope you enjoyed learning about Mount Rushmore's history. Come visit us soon!

Mount Rushmore Facts

❧ Thomas Jefferson's face was originally carved on George Washington's right. Unfortunately, the rock had cracks in it. After 18 months of carving, the workers blasted Jefferson's face from the mountain with dynamite. Then they carved his face on Washington's left.

❧ Abraham Lincoln's head was never completed. Money ran out for the project, because the U.S. government was sending money to England to help it fight in World War II (1939–1945).

Glossary

Civil War — (1861–1865) the battle between states in the North and South that led to the end of slavery in the United States

Declaration of Independence — a document written by Thomas Jefferson in 1776; it declares the United States a free and independent country and says that every U.S. citizen has rights that the government should protect

dedication — a ceremony marking the official completion or opening of a building or monument

democracy — a form of government with equal rights and privileges

granite — a hard, gray type of rock

Lakota Sioux — a Native American tribe from North and South Dakota

symbol — an object that stands for something else

U.S. Constitution — the plan for how the U.S. government works

Index

To Learn More

More Books to Read

Bauer, Marion Dane. *Mount Rushmore.*
New York: Aladdin Paperbacks, 2007.

Jango-Cohen, Judith. *Mount Rushmore.*
Minneapolis: Lerner Publications Co., 2004.

Patrick, Jean L.S. *Who Carved the Mountain?*
The Story of Mount Rushmore. Keystone,
S.D.: Mount Rushmore History
Association, 2005.

On the Web

FactHound offers a safe, fun way to find
educator-approved Internet sites related to this book.

Here's what you do:

1. Visit *www.facthound.com*
2. Choose your grade level.
3. Begin your search.

This book's ID number is 9781404851689

Look for all of the books in the *American Symbols* series:

24

Author and Illustrator

Thomas Kingsley Troupe is a
freelance writer, filmmaker, and
firefighter/EMT. He is the author
of a children's reader, *Patrick's
Super Socks*, and also enjoys
writing young adult novels. His
love of action and adventure is
often reflected in his stories and
films. Thomas lives in Minnesota
with his wife and young son.

Matthew Skeens graduated
from the Minneapolis College
of Art and Design with a BFA
in illustration. When he's not
drawing, Matthew likes to run,
solve mysteries, chase bears,
and pogo stick up stairs (but
not down). He lives in Des
Moines, Iowa, with his wife,
Heather, and their orange
cat named Calvin.